Now I Know

Animals at Night

Written by Sharon Peters
Illustrated by Paul Harvey

Troll Associates

Library of Congress Cataloging in Publication Data

Peters, Sharon.
   Animals at night.

   (Now I know)
   Summary: Text and illustrations describe various noc-
turnal animals and their habits.
   1. Nocturnal animals—Juvenile literature. [1. Noc-
turnal animals] I. Harvey, Paul, 1926-   ill.
II. Title.
QL755.5.P46   1983   591.5   82-19226
ISBN 0-89375-903-1

10   9   8   7   6   5   4   3   2   1

The sun is going down.

Night is coming.

Out goes the light.

Good night!

Hey! Who is there?

Who is outside tonight?

Many animals are just waking up.

Night is when they work and play.

Look up in the tree.

Who is there?

Those large eyes belong
to the owl.

The owl sits quietly on the branch,
looking and waiting.

It is looking for something to eat.

Who else is in the tree?
Look there.

The opossum is hanging from the branch by its tail.

It is having something to eat.

In the summer, fireflies fill the night air.

Whoosh! There goes a bat.

Bats are good fliers, even in the dark.

They catch and eat dinner while they are flying!

Who is there?
Dark eyes are looking out into the night.

It's a raccoon.

Raccoons eat many kinds of food—even garbage!

Let's go down to the pond.

Croak!
That big noise is coming from
this little animal.

That is how the bullfrog sings.
Its neck puffs up like a balloon.

Splash! The beavers are going for a swim.

They are good swimmers.

Tonight, they are making a new home
from branches and mud.

Tonight, there are many animals at work and play.